grades 5-6
Fall 1990

DAVID
THE STORY OF A KING

Lillie Patterson

Illustration by Charles Cox

Abingdon Press

Nashville

David: The Story of a King

Copyright © 1985 by Abingdon Press

All Rights Reserved

Library of Congress in Publication Data

PATTERSON, LILLIE.
  David, the story of a king.
  Summary: A retelling of the Old Testament story of David the
shepherd who became King of Israel.
  1. David, King of Israel—Juvenile literature.
  2. Palestine—Kings and rulers—Biography—Juvenile literature.
  3. Bible. O.T.—Biography—Juvenile literature [1. David, King of
Israel. 2. Bible stories—O.T.]
  I. Title.
  BS580.D3P34   1985   222'.40924 [B]   84-24210

ISBN 0-687-10280-4

Manufactured in the United States of America

Contents

To the memory of my grandmother
Cornelia Patterson Green
who read to me
and opened my mind and heart
to the magic of words and music

1.

The Shepherd

The first light of day tinged the skies above the hills around Bethlehem, in Judah. Even in the early dawn the landscape was breathtaking. Orchards of deep-green olive trees stood sedately in rows, heavy with fruit to be pressed into oil. Grapevines flourished to promise a plentiful supply of wine. And off in the distance, cornfields and barley fields waved the coming harvest of food.

Jesse, a farmer in Bethlehem, stirred with the dawn. His day began as always with family prayers, for Jesse was a very religious man.

By the time the sun arched beyond the rim of the rugged hills, all family members were at their daily tasks. For a farm family in Bethlehem in the 1000s B.C., there was abundant work for sons and daughters of all ages. There were eight strong sons in the family of Jesse the farmer. The youngest son was David.

To David ben Jesse, David the son of Jesse, fell the task of herding the sheep. Bethlehem farmers were famed for raising prized sheep and the task was often given to one of the younger sons.

So David, barely in his teens, prepared to tend the flock for the day. He filled a bottle made of goatskins with fresh milk for his lunch. Fresh-baked bread, cheese, and raisins rounded out the hearty meals.

DAVID

The shepherd slung the strap of his woolen sling around his shoulder and picked up his staff with one hand. With the other hand he carried a lyre, an instrument of the harp family.

Then David drove the bleating sheep to the upland pasture to find food. He located a spot where there were tufts of grass and shrubs, and the animals could use their grinding teeth like sharp-edged blades. A nearby rocky spring provided water.

With the sheep settled and grazing, David looked forward to several hours of solitude. The sheep would need him only when they strayed, or when danger threatened. For some young men the life of a shepherd proved lonely and monotonous.

With David it was different. He used the hours to create poems and songs. Years of practice on the harp had given him the skill to coax rich tones from the many-stringed instrument.

The shepherd braced his body against a low hillock, sitting in full view of the flock. Resting the harp lightly against his chest, he ran his nimble fingers across the strings in aimless chords.

David ben Jesse sang.

His voice rose higher and higher, blending words and music until they circled the sun-scorched hills with a rainbow of sounds. He sang to celebrate the majesty of the earth and the beauty of all things dwelling upon it.

> Mountains and all hills,
> > fruit trees and all cedars!
> Beasts and all cattle,
> > creeping things and flying birds!
> Kings of the earth and all peoples,
> > princes and rulers of the earth!
> Young men and maidens together,
> > old men and children!
> Let them praise the name of the Lord!
> > Psalm 148:9-13

As David played, his almond-shaped eyes swept the landscape, searching for any hint of danger. His handsome face looked as though the features might have been chiseled by an unerring sculptor, with dark hair catching the glint of the sun in a reddish cast.

Suddenly there was silence in the pasture. The singing stopped. David's fingers stilled his harp strings. His eyes, trained to note the slightest changes, watched more intently.

Danger. David sensed it instinctively. Trouble was coming to the peaceful Bethlehem hills. The leaves on distant bushes moved ever so slightly. The trouble moved on silent, padded paws.

The shepherd sprang to his feet, eyes, legs, hands, mind, all moving in coordinated rhythm. Holding his heavy staff and sling ready, he ran to meet the danger that threatened his sheep.

He saw the lion. The huge beast, hungry for food, stalked toward the unsuspecting flock.

David moved as confidently as the lion. At the moment the lion snatched a little lamb to devour it, the shepherd was at the spot. Raising his heavy staff high, he brought it down upon the lion's head with all his might. Again and again he crashed downward with the staff, fighting as fiercely as the lion. With one last crushing blow, David killed the beast and rescued the sheep.

David smiled with relief and satisfaction. This was his job, to protect his flock. Danger came from small animals as well as the large ones. For the smaller creepy-crawly creatures, such as snakes and lizards, David fitted a stone into his sling, aimed, and let fly. The day-to-day use of his slingstone had made him an expert marksman.

So it was, day to day. In the silent loneliness of the

hills, David dreamed. And he fashioned his dreams into creative patterns of words and rhythm.

He sang his own songs. And he sang those that had been popular for centuries among his people, the Israelites. Old or new, his favorite songs told of the glory of God and the beauty of the earth and all things, great and small.

> All sheep and oxen,
>   and also the beasts of the field,
> the birds of the air,
>   and the fish of the sea,
> whatever passes along the paths
>   of the sea.

Psalm 8:7-8

News about David and his skill with the harp and the slingstone spread beyond Bethlehem. People who had never seen him heard about him.

David the bold shepherd,
David the skilled harpist,
David the sweet singer,
David the expert with the slingstone.

2.

A Noble Heritage

Every year Jesse of Bethlehem journeyed with his family to make a holy pilgrimage. They came to the religious center where the Ark of the Covenant was once kept. The story of the Ark stretched far back into Hebrew history. These accounts intertwined with deeds of heroes and heroines, defeats and conquests, hardships and triumphs.

Jesse made sure that his young son knew the

significance of his history, and David learned it well.
The stories began with Abraham, the first patriarch of
the Hebrews:

There lived in the city of Ur, an ancient city on the
Euphrates River, an upright man named Abram. He
was well advanced in years, when one day he heard
the voice of God calling to him.

"Go from your country and your kindred
and your father's house
to the land that I will show you.
And I will make of you a great nation,
And I will bless you, and make your name great
so that you will be a blessing.
I will bless those who bless you,
And him who curses you I will curse;
and by you all the families of the earth
shall bless themselves."

Genesis 12:1-3

Abram took his household and goods and flocks,
traveling until he came to Canaan, lying between the
Jordan River and the Mediterranean Sea.

Later in Canaan Abram heard the voice of God:

"Lift up your eyes, and look
from the place where you are,
northward and southward and eastward and
westward;
for all the land which you see
I will give to you
and to your descendants for ever."

Genesis 13:14-15

When Abram was ninety-nine years old, he had
another vision. This time God spoke to him and gave
him a new name.

"No longer shall your name be Abram,
but your name
shall be Abraham,
for I have made you
the father of a multitude of nations."

Genesis 17:5

The name Abraham means "father of a multitude." His wife's name was changed from Sarai to Sarah, meaning "princess." God also told Abraham that Sarah would give birth to a son, even though she was an elderly woman. The baby boy was born to Abraham and Sarah the next spring. They named him Isaac, which means "laughter." And Isaac had twin sons, Jacob and Esau. As the boys grew up, Esau became bold and honorable. Jacob had to struggle between his good nature and his evil tendencies. After he cheated Esau out of his birthright, he was forced to leave home for fear that his brother would kill him.

One night as Jacob slept beneath the stars, he dreamed he saw a ladder stretching from the earth up beyond the stars. This time Jacob had the vision and heard the voice of God telling him that all his children would be blessed. From that night Jacob's good side ruled his life. He made peace with his brother.

Later in life Jacob crossed the Jordan River and came to Canaan, the land of his birth, the land given to Abraham. There the Lord appeared to him once more: "Your name is Jacob; no longer shall your name be called Jacob, but Israel shall be your name."

Jacob, or Israel, had twelve sons. Of them all he loved Joseph best. His brothers were so jealous of this that one day they secretly sold Joseph to a caravan, and he was taken to Egypt as a slave. In Egypt, Joseph rose to a high position. He later sent for his father and brothers who came with all their people to live in Egypt.

They prospered and increased in numbers over the years. When a new pharaoh came to power, however, they were forced into slave labor. For years the descendants of Jacob, known as the children of Israel, labored in bondage.

01616

Finally Moses guided them out of Egypt in a daring escape. After years of wandering in the desert wilderness, the Israelites came to the majestic mountain of Sinai. Moses climbed up the slopes and disappeared into the clouds.

When the leader came down, he brought the Ten Commandments—rules to guide daily living in the new homeland—written on tablets of stone. An Ark, a special chest, was fashioned to hold the tablets of stone. The chest was lined and covered with gold, with a golden angel guarding each end. The cover of the Ark became known as the Mercy Seat, and the Ark of the Covenant was looked upon as a symbol of the presence of God.

Finally, after more years of hardships and travel, the tribes of Israel arrived in Canaan, the Promised Land. Their troubles were not over. There were other tribes living in Canaan, warlike people. The Israelites had to fight for a foothold. And many times when they fought, the Ark of the Covenant was carried before them.

The land that they held was divided among the twelve tribes. Each tribe had been named for one of the twelve sons of Jacob, renamed Israel. David ben Jesse was of the tribe of Judah, a tribe with its own heroes and heroines.

David's great-grandmother was Ruth. Her story made her one of the best loved women of the ages:

Once there was a famine in Bethlehem. A man named Elimelech took his wife, Naomi, and his sons, Mahlon and Chilion, from Bethlehem to search for food. They came to the country of Moab. While in Moab, Elimelech died. The two sons grew up and married girls from Moab. Chilion married Orpah, and Mahlon married Ruth. Then tragedy struck. First, one of Naomi's sons died, then the other. She was left a childless widow in a strange land. Naomi decided to return to her homeland. She said to her two daughters-in law, "Go, return each of you to her mother's house."

Orpah obeyed, kissing Naomi goodbye. But Ruth clung to Naomi, pleading to go along. "For where you go I will go," Ruth said, "and where you lodge I will lodge; your people shall be my people, and your God my God." So the two went to Bethlehem. They arrived at the time of the barley harvest. According to an old Hebrew custom, poor people were permitted to glean in the fields behind the reapers, picking up grain left behind.

Ruth went to gather stalks of barley so that they could eat. It happened that the field belonged to a rich landowner named Boaz, who was a kinsman of Naomi's husband. He was impressed with the generous spirit of the beautiful foreign woman. The wealthy farmer persuaded Ruth to marry him.

Ruth and Boaz had a son named Obed. And Obed became the father of Jesse, who was the father of David. So behind the shepherd of Bethlehem stretched a rich historic tapestry, with color and drama to give themes to a thousand songs.

David strummed his harp and let his imagination soar.

3.

A Shepherd Plays for a King

During the days of David's youth, Israel appointed a king. His name was Saul.

Until Saul's reign, the Israelites were advised by Judges. Samuel was the last of these ruler-judges. He was a prophet, priest, judge, and ruler, and he believed that God spoke to the people through him.

One day the people came to Samuel and spoke their wishes. Their lives were constantly threatened by enemy tribes. Many times families were forced to leave their homes and hide among rocks and inside caves to stay alive. So they asked Samuel to appoint a single national leader, a king who would organize a strong army for protection.

And Samuel chose Saul, son of Kish, of the tribe of Benjamin.

Saul was tall, with a commanding appearance. Like most men of his tribe, he was skilled in using the sling and the bow. He was also a master at planning surprise attacks, and guerilla raids. There was no standing army as such, but each tribe contributed men to fight when needed. The new king united these valiant men into a strong fighting force. All went well until an unfortunate misunderstanding arose between Samuel, the religious leader, and Saul, the king and military leader because of two incidents. Once, before an important battle, King Saul waited for Samuel to come and conduct the usual religious sacrifices to God and to ask God's blessing during the fighting. As days passed and his warriors began to leave, the king in desperation conducted the services himself—a ritual reserved for priests and Levites, members of the tribe of Levi. Samuel finally arrived and berated the king. "Your kingdom shall not continue," the prophet foretold. "The Lord has sought out a man after his own heart."

The second incident came about during a conflict with the fierce and troublesome Amalekites. Samuel directed Saul to kill every man, woman, and child among these enemy attackers—even the animals. The Amalekites had tried to stop the Israelites during their flight from Egypt to Canaan, and Samuel believed that God wanted Saul to destroy completely such enemies.

Saul disobeyed and spared the life of Agag, the king of the Amalekites. He also saved the best of the sheep and cattle. In his fury over this disobedience to him, and to God as he deemed it, Samuel heaped a curse upon the head of King Saul, even though the king pleaded for forgiveness. The Lord, Samuel decreed, had rejected Saul as king over Israel!

As Samuel turned to leave, the king tried to grab his robe to detain him, still begging forgiveness. The robe tore in his hand. Samuel then turned to the king with a final, more dooming sentence: "The Lord has torn the kingdom of Israel from you this day, and has given it to a neighbor of yours, who is a better man."

Saul's spirit was crushed by this judgment. Worse, the religious leader refused to see or to speak to the king. Samuel grieved and prayed for Saul, but he never showed forgiveness. And from that day, the personality of the king began to change. He acted as though he believed God had truly rejected him.

The king became moody and depressed. Some days he sat for hours, not speaking nor showing interest in life about him. Other times he exploded in fits of rage. The army captains and the offices of the king's court were at a loss to explain or to help. An evil spirit must have taken hold of the king's mind, they said. Nobody knew how to help him. They began to ask about a possible cure. What magic would be potent enough to exorcise the evil spirit and make the king himself again?

Music.

Music was the answer. It had the power to heal the mind and heart. So the people of King Saul's court looked around for someone who could play the lyre or harp. They well knew that the gentlest, most beautiful music could be played upon these instruments.

It happened that an officer at the court came from Bethlehem. He told about the young shepherd who could play the harp and could make up songs as well. "He is David, the son of Jesse," the soldier reported. The king's messengers hastened to Bethlehem to find David. They found him in the pastures with his sheep. David's father was proud to send a son to help the king. He prepared loaves of bread, a bottle of wine, and a prized kid goat as a present for Saul.

David prepared his precious harp for the trip. He gathered an armful of blue lilies and twisted the stems around each of the strings. The lilies protected the strings from the damaging heat of the sun and kept them from snapping.

So the shepherd from Bethlehem arrived at the court of King Saul. David went before the king, stopping about ten paces from the royal seat. Then he knelt and offered his gifts and music. King Saul looked upon the youth from Bethlehem. David was not tall, but his appearance and the confidence with which he carried himself gave a sense of strength. The sun and the outdoor life had bronzed his skin to a rich almond-colored hue. His complexion blended beautifully with his dark hair, polished by a reddish sheen.

David played. And he sang. He sangs songs of comfort and of compassion for the tormented king.

> Therefore we will not fear
>   though the earth should change,
> though the mountains shake
>   in the heart of the sea;
> though its waters roar and foam,
>   though the mountains tremble
>   with its tumult . . .
>   Be still,
>   and know that I am God.
>
> Psalm 46:2-3, 10

That was the beginning. Each day when moods of depression or fits of rage came upon the king, David brought his harp to play and sing. His voice and his instrument highlighted the beauty of the old songs. The music of David, the shepherd, brought to the king a measure of calm. He acted his old self again.

So after a while David returned to his father's farm in Bethlehem. He returned to sheepherding, and dreaming, and making up songs. Now his dreams and his songs embraced a wider sphere. For a brief period, he had caught a glimpse of life at the court of King Saul.

4.

A Duel with a Giant

Accounts of the combat evolved into timeless legacy. For centuries poets and storytellers, artists and dramatists recaptured the thrill of the struggle. The story gives courage to the fainthearted, boldness to the underdog, and hope to all who single-handedly fight despite impossible odds.

The story recalls the day when David dueled a giant.

The blare of ram's-horn trumpets called the soldiers of King Saul for war. The Philistines were upon them again. Of all the enemy tribes that surrounded Israel, the Philistines were the most persistent. They seemed determined to drive the Israelites from their new homeland.

On his father's farm in Bethlehem, David longed to answer the ram's-horn call. King Saul looked for strong, valiant men to join his fighting host. David's three oldest brothers had already joined the king's army, but he was still needed to care for his father's sheep.

One day, however, David's father called to him. His brothers were in need of food, Jesse told his son. David must go to the army camp and take some battle ration. At this time there was no treasury to support their army. Strong men left their farms and herds and other pursuits when they were needed to fight. Their families supplied them with food.

David prepared to go, anticipating the sight of a great battle. His father packed a quantity of parched grain, loaves of bread, and ten cheeses. Along with these he placed a goatskin bottle filled with wine.

Early the next morning David left his sheep in the care of another keeper. Then he prepared to leave.

"See how your brothers fare," his father told him, "and bring some token from them."

David promised, and went on his way. He reached the encampment as the soldiers lined up for battle, army against army. The Philistines camped on a low, oak-covered mountain ridge. King Saul's forces faced them from the opposite ridge. A valley stretched between.

David left the rations in charge of the baggage keeper and went to find his brothers. As he stood talking with them he looked toward the enemy camp. An amazing spectacle left him speechless. Out from the Philistine camp strode a colossal soldier, a giant. He was called Goliath, David learned. He came from the city-state of Gath in Philistia. Goliath, the Philistine champion, came out each day to defy the soldiers of Israel.

The giant stood on the ridge like a towering cedar tree. When he stretched to his full height, he measured nine feet, nine inches tall. The brass helmet on his massive head gleamed in the sunlight. A heavy bronze-plate armor protected his gigantic body. His huge hand held a spear as stout as a length of timber. His shield bearer went before him. Goliath the giant turned and faced the soldiers of the king's army. His voice rolled like heavy thunder as he hurled a challenge across the valley.

"Why have you come out to draw up for battle?" he taunted. "Am I not a Philistine, and are you not servants of Saul? Choose a man for yourselves and let him come down to me"

Silence.

Goliath repeated the dare, this time making it more threatening. "Choose a man for yourselves. If he is able to fight with me and kill me, then we will be your servants; but if I prevail against him and kill him, then you shall be our servants, and serve me." The giant kept up the taunting. "I defy the ranks of Israel this day. Give me a man, that we may fight together."

David watched, and listened, and thought of a plan. He took the plan to King Saul. "Let no man's heart fail," he told the king. "Your servant will go and fight the Philistine giant."

The king's words revealed his doubts. "You are not able to go against this Philistine to fight with him. You are but a youth, and he has been a man of war from his youth."

The shepherd looked up at the king. Then David told the story of the day when he faced a ferocious lion that threatened his sheep. He recalled how he fought bears and other creatures to protect his flock. David spoke quietly, but with confidence. "The Lord who delivered me from the paw of the lion and from the paw of the bear, will deliver me from the hand of this Philistine."

"Go," the king said to David, "and the Lord go with you."

David the shepherd prepared to battle the giant. He refused the offer of a heavy coat of armor or a brass helmet. Nor did he want an armor-bearer to walk before him, carrying a shield.

Instead, David chose to wear his simple shepherd's tunic. He ran down to a nearby flowing stream and searched for stones; five smooth stones. These he dropped into the shepherd's bag he wore around his shoulder. He tightened his grip on his sling, used so many times to protect the sheep. With his sling and five smooth stones the shepherd stepped forward to fight the giant.

David strode down to the valley while onlookers watched in awe. His music and poetry gave a natural sense of rhythm to his movements. The years of walking the hills and meadows gave a lightness to his bearing, so that he stepped with the lightness of a temple dancer. Goliath lumbered forward to meet the youth. He noted that his challenger carried no sword, and wore no fighting armor.

"Am I a dog," Goliath bellowed, "that you come to me with sticks?"

David moved closer to his foe, head high, eyes fearless. "Come to me," the giant roared. "I will give your flesh to the fowls of the air, and the beasts of the field."

David moved steadily nearer, speaking in a calm voice. "You come to me with a sword and with a spear and with a javelin: but I come to you in the name of the Lord of hosts, the God of the armies of Israel, whom you have defied." The giant's roar shook the earth under David's feet. Goliath lunged toward him, hoping to finish him off with one mighty blow.

The shepherd, nimble of foot, moved away quickly.

In the next moment he fitted one smooth stone into his sling. The giant charged again.

David stepped back, whirled the sling above his head, and aimed. Swift and sure he aimed, pinpointing the spot on the giant's head not protected by armor. Then he let the stone fly. It struck Goliath near the eye where his armor could not protect him.

For one still, incredible moment, the giant stood stiff and upright. A look of disbelief froze on his face. Then slowly, like a tremendous tree brought to earth, he toppled face-forward, stunned by the impact of the stone. The heavy armor clanged as the giant hit the earth.

Before the giant could recover, David ran, snatched the giant's own sword, and cut off his head. Goliath, the champion of the Philistines, was dead.

At the frightening sight, the Philistines began to scatter. The jubilant soldiers of King Saul's army pursued them through the hills—all the way back to their home in Philistia.

And David, who slayed a giant, was hailed as a hero.

5.

David and Jonathan

"Let David remain in my service, for he has found favor in my sight."

Jesse of Bethlehem received the request brought by messengers of King Saul. Although his son was needed on the farm, the Bethlehemite willingly sent him into the king's service. David's days on the landscape tending sheep came to a close. He left to live in the royal house of King Saul.

The king ruled from his native hill town of Gibeah. His home could not be termed a castle. It was built more as a roughhewn fortress. The house of stone stood like a sentinel high atop a hill, guarding the town.

To David, accustomed to life in a small farmhouse, or in a pasture, the fortress-home became a castle in his mind. On the first level a huge common room provided space where the people of the court could assemble. On rainy or chilly days, King Saul held court there. Most other times he held court out of doors under a tamarisk tree.

The upper level of the house accommodated spaces for sleeping. One large area was used for storing weapons. There David could examine the sharp-tipped spears, the swords, the slings, and the varied designs of bows and arrows.

To this home King Saul brought David and treated him as one of his own sons. The simple shepherd's tunics were laid aside. David began to dress in clothes of fine linen for warm weather and of pure wool for the cold. His ready smile and winning ways captivated the king and practically everyone in the household. The royal family presented an interesting contrast of features and personalities. There were several sons, and the oldest of them was Jonathan. There were also two daughters, lovely and high-spirited girls. The oldest daughter was named Merab, and the youngest was named Michal.

The isolated shepherd's life had given David little opportunity to form friendships outside his own family. It was at the court of King Saul that he met the best friend he would ever know: Prince Jonathan!

For David and Jonathan it was instant friendship at first sight. Jonathan was much older than David, but the two were of a kindred spirit. The king's oldest son had proven himself a fearless warrior. Yet he had the same kind of sensitive and compassionate nature as the young shepherd.

The news that reached David's ears about Jonathan's bravery in battle increased his admiration for the prince. Jonathan's skill with the bow and arrow matched David's skill with the slingstone. When the prince was not engaged in warfare, he spent hours in the fields, practicing the art of speeding arrows toward targets with deadly accuracy. Whenever the king went into battle his oldest son was usually by his side.

One story the people told about Jonathan came about during another skirmish with the Philistines. This time the long-time foes had camped on a steep hill. Prince Jonathan and his armor-bearer crept between two steep, jagged rocks to spy upon them.

Jonathan decided to try a daring trick to make the Philistines think a large army was coming. "It may be that the Lord will work for us," he whispered to his armor-bearer.

"Do all that your mind inclines to, I am with you," his faithful companion answered.

The two men inched near the garrison of the Philistines. Then they let out wild war cries, as though they were part of a host of fighters. The enemies were indeed tricked. "Look, the Hebrews are coming out of the holes where they have hid themselves," they called out. They believed that a large army hid behind the rocks.

The Philistines panicked. Jonathan and his armor-bearer rushed in with shouts, confusing them. Other Israelites dashed from their hiding places among the rocks and joined the fracas. The enemies began dashing hither and thither, fighting among themselves. By the time they learned the truth, King Saul and his army arrived to defeat them.

A sequel to this story provided David with an insight into the characters of both the king and the prince. After the battle the soldiers were tired and hungry, but the king ordered that they must fast until nightfall. "Cursed be the man who eats food until it is evening," he warned. The soldiers knew that the king would not hesitate to kill any of them who disobeyed this order. As they passed under an overhanging tree, they came upon a honeycomb dripping sweetness. The soldiers held their mouths closed lest any of it drip upon their lips.

But the prince did not know of his father's order. When Jonathan passed under the honeycomb, he reached out a stick and touched the sweetness to his lips.

King Saul learned of this and his rage was fearsome to see. Jonathan, though his own son, must die.

The prince stepped before his father. "Here I am," he said in his quiet way. "I will die."

The soldiers saved him, for they loved the prince. "Shall Jonathan die, Jonathan who has won this great victory in Israel? Far from it. As the Lord lives, there shall not one hair of his head fall to the ground."

Small wonder David admired the prince. The two became inseparable friends. One day they decided to enter into a binding covenant of friendship.

Following the custom of the times, the friends took a vow of loyalty and comradeship. True to the tradition in their country, David and Jonathan exchanged clothing and weapons. Jonathan took off his garments, even the expensive, embroidered girdle he wore around his waist. All these he gave to David. After that he gave him his bow and arrow. In the same manner David gave the prince the clothing he wore and handed him his slingstone. By this symbolic gesture the two signified that whatever one of them owned in

life would always belong to the other. Together, they repeated an oath, binding them as friends for all time.

"We will protect each other in time of danger. We will care for each other in time of need. Always and forever we will remain loyal friends." The two friends embraced and sealed the agreement with a kiss.

Both Jonathan and David knew that the brother-like friendship might be tested in time to come. But the two strong characters also knew that they had courage and faith in each other to pass any test. They knew the meaning of the word used to describe the bond of friendship that bound them. It was known as *hesed*: steadfast love.

6.

The Warrior-Poet

In the beginning David's chief duty at the court was to play music for the king. As royal harpist he was on call at all times. Whenever King Saul's moods of depression required the medicine of music, David came running with his harp.

Now that David's world had widened, the themes for his songs had become more varied. He wrote some of his song-poems to praise King Saul. Other poems honored significant events—victory in battle, happiness on feast days, the beauty of sheepshearing .

Some of David's songs were as old as the hills of Bethlehem. And some were as recent as a newborn lamb. The words he sang to the accompaniment of his harp painted tranquil scenes for times when the king raged. So clearly did David paint the scenes that even the tormented king could see them.

> The hills gird themselves with joy,
> the meadows clothe themselves with flocks,
> the valleys deck themselves with grain,
> they shout and sing together for joy.

Psalm 65:12-13

Through songs David reminded King Saul of their noble heritage. Israel had endured hardships and resisted foes for centuries. Yet the nation had survived. And the king had played a key part in this courageous history.

> When Israel went forth from Egypt;
> the house of Jacob
> from a people of strange language,
> Judah became his sanctuary,
> Israel his dominion.
> The sea looked and fled,
> Jordan turned back.
> The mountains skipped like rams,
> the hills like lambs.

Psalm 114:1-4

The melody-maker shared his music with the servants and with the royal family alike. He used music to entertain the soldiers. Many nights he visited with them as they sat beneath the stars beside their goats' hair tents. The strings of his harp and the lilt of his honey-toned voice would bring moments of cheer to otherwise wearisome hours.

David now had a chance to get a closer look at the king's fighting host, and he set for himself another goal. One by one, he would master the skill of all the fighting weapons. From his shepherd days he had already mastered the sling. He could hurl shots with his right hand, then, in a lightning second, switch and hurl with his left. Now instead of using the slingshot to chase animals from sheep, he practiced using it to shower death-dealing stones upon enemies. Each day the range of his shots grew longer.

So as David grew into manhood, a new interest competed for his time and energies. The life of a warrior challenged his adventurous spirit. Besides this, he knew that warriors were held in high esteem.

His big moment came unexpectedly. King Saul appointed him to be his royal armor-bearer. This was a high honor for the one-time shepherd. Many seasoned soldiers coveted the honor of carrying the king's weapons into battle and walking before him.

As armor-bearer David continued to learn more about weapons. He learned to hurl a spear with such force that the spear tip would pin a victim against a wall or a tree, or hold him fast to the earth. He soon knew how to wield a sharp-edged sword as easily as he had struck blows with his stout shepherd's staff.

In this manner David trained for his vital role of helping to defend his homeland. Israel was hemmed in by alien tribes, and David knew that the existence of the nation would depend upon skill in battle for years to come.

King Saul recognized David's progress and rewarded him by making him a captain over a small force of about three hundred fighters. These small companies were very important because they were called upon in emergencies when a little village or town was suddenly beset by an unexpected raid.

Wherever David went, in army tent or royal house, his harp was ever present. Words and music remained his first love. For the poet-warrior, none of his interests detracted from the others. In fact, each could enhance the high quality of the others.

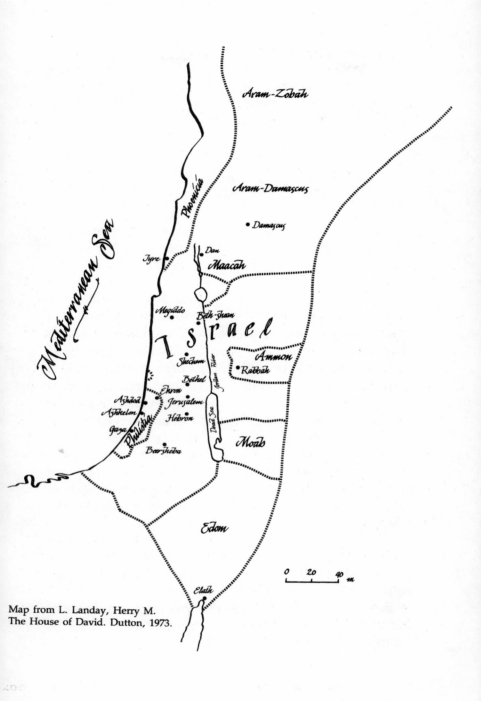

Aram-Zobah

Aram-Damascus

• Damascus

Mediterranean Sea

Phoenicia

Tyre

Dan

Maacah

Megiddo

Beth-Shean

Israel

Shechem

Ammon

Bethel

• Rabbah

Ekron

Ashdod
Ashkelon

Jerusalem

Philistia

Hebron

Gaza

Jordan River

Dead Sea

Moab

Beersheba

Edom

0   20   40 m

Elath

Map from L. Landay, Herry M.
The House of David. Dutton, 1973.

David sang of this:

> Blessed be the Lord, my rock
> who trains my hands for war,
> and my fingers for battle.
>
> Psalm 144:1

7.

Michal

Michal, the youngest daughter of King Saul was fair and well favored. When she dressed in her gowns of scarlet and gold, with earrings and armlets, she dazzled the court.

Michal fell in love with David ben Jesse.

This was not surprising. All Israel seemed to love David. And as people will do with heroes, they began to make up songs and legends about the handsome young soldier-singer.

At first it pleased King Saul to see David receive so much praise and admiration. The king loved him too. But as this adulation mounted, the king began to wonder. Was David receiving too much attention? King Saul did not have to wait long for an answer.

One day David and the king returned from a battle in which their army had won an astounding victory. Along with their warriors they marched home joyfully, celebrating their good fortune.

In towns and cities along the way, the women came out to meet the homecoming heroes. They came with tamborines, dancing and singing.

One song was new. The women sang it in a call-and-response manner that was popular at festival celebrations.

One group began the chant:

"Saul has slain his thousands,"

The other group responded:

"And David his ten thousands."

Over and over the singers and dancers repeated the song:

"Saul has slain his thousands,

And David his ten thousands."

The king listened to the song, and his anger mounted with each repetition. The song struck at his heart as though each singer had aimed a dart instead of joyful words. And he said, "They have ascribed to David ten thousands, and to me they have ascribed thousands; and what more can he have but the kingdom?"

From that day on the king kept a jealous eye on the young man he had once loved so much. David was growing too popular, he decided. The people seemed to be transferring to David the love they once held for the king.

King Saul recalled the dreadful prophecy spoken to him by Samuel at their last meeting. Was David the man who would take his kingdom from him? The man after God's own heart?

This anger and jealousy brought on the king's mental sickness again. The alternating moods of deep depression and violent rage came as before.

One day the king sat in his royal seat, his hand gripping a spear. This was a familiar pose. For hours he sat in the same position, deep in one of his sullen moods.

David received his familiar summons. Come and bring your harp. Come to sing for the king.

The harpist glided into the room with tiger-quiet steps. He did not speak, but his eyes swept over the room. He sensed danger, the way he once felt danger in the pasture when the sheep were threatened.

David sat on the floor, facing the king. As he played his harp his voice poured out a familiar refrain, half speaking, half singing. Words and music dropped into the room like the gentle falling of showers on a parched cornfield.

The king watched the singer with unnerving intensity, but David kept on singing and watching the king. By now he realized that the affection King Saul once felt for him had turned to a feeling akin to hate.

The danger came without warning. King Saul gripped the spear tighter, then in a sudden motion, he hurled the weapon at David's head.

Quick reflexes spelled the difference between life and death. David ducked. Had he not done so, the spear would have pinned his body to the wall. Instead, it missed him by a whisper and trembled as it struck the wall.

David fled from the wrath of the king. He knew that he must escape from that wrath before it destroyed him. He ran to find his best friend, who also happened to be the king's favorite son.

Jonathan helped David to weigh the options open to him. David felt he should leave quickly. Jonathan begged him to stay. With his father ill, he needed David, as a friend and as a warrior.

The two friends worked out a plan. Jonathan promised to persuade the king to place David in charge of one of the units going away to fight the Philistines. Perhaps by the time he returned the king's mood would have changed.

David left. His campaigns against the Philistines were so victorious that they brought him even greater acclaim. New songs were sung to praise him.

When he returned home, David made a bold decision regarding his personal life. Encouraged by Jonathan, he decided to ask King Saul for permission to marry Michal. Jonathan spoke with his father about the match, reminding him how perfect the union would be.

To the amazement of David and Jonathan, the king readily gave his consent to the marriage. He had his secret reasons. "Let me give her to him," he said. "Let her be the snare that lures him to his death at the hand of the Philistines."

The king agreed, but David had his doubts. He was popular, but he was poor. He had not accumulated the wealth of farms and vineyards and herds owned by many other warriors. He lacked gold or silver to give as a dowry for his bride.

King Saul had a ready answer. He did not want wealth as a dowry. He wanted proof that David had killed one hundred Philistine soldiers in battle. Once again he hoped that David would be killed in the fighting.

David took a company of his men and slew the one hundred Philistines. Then he killed another one hundred to double the number the king requested.

The king had no choice but to keep his word. David and Michal were married, to the delight of Israel and Judah. The joy could not be shared by King Saul. Everything seemed to go right for David, as though he lived a charmed life. More and more the king thought about the words of Prophet Samuel.

"God who is the splendor of Israel does not deceive or change his mind. The Lord will give the kingdom of Israel to a better man than you." So had Samuel spoken. Now King Saul made up his mind. David must die!

8.

The Escape

The king set the plan in motion.

His messengers, who also served as guards, were sent to surround David's house and keep watch. The moment David tried to leave they were to seize him and take him to the king.

That was the plan. However, one of the messengers whispered the plan to Michal, and Michal whispered it to her husband. "If you do not save your life tonight, tomorrow you will be killed," she said.

There was no time to hesitate. They sent word to Jonathan, and the three worked out a plan of escape. They also decided upon a temporary hiding place for David.

That night, under cover of darkness, Michal helped her husband to climb down through a small window in the back of the house. As a shepherd David had learned the art of moving stealthily. He melted into the night without making a sound.

Inside the house Michal worked to give him time. She took a statue of one of their household gods and placed it in their bed. Around the head of the statue she arranged a rug made of goats' hair. Lying under the cover in the dark, the statue looked as though it could have been a person asleep in the bed.

Next morning when David failed to appear as usual at his doorway, the king's men rushed inside the house. Michal was ready for them. David, her husband, was very ill, she explained. He could not possibly leave his bed. As she spoke she wept uncontrollably. She was crying over David and his plight. The men assumed that her sorrow was due to his illness.

The messengers explained David's sickness to the king. Suspecting a plot, King Saul shouted another order. "Bring him up to me in the bed, that I may kill him."

By this time David had found a hiding place in the woods. The king's men found only the statue in the bed, with the goats' hair rug around its head.

The king sent for Michal. "Why have you deceived me?" he asked his daughter. "Why did you let my enemy go, so that he has escaped?"

Michal, quick thinking as ever, had a ready reply. Her husband had forced her to help him, she said. Had she refused, she told her father, her desperate husband might have killed her.

Michal had done her part. It was now up to Jonathan to find David and help him. They still were not certain that the king would not change his mind about killing David. Perhaps the cloud over his mind would lift, they hoped, and he would realize that David was not a threat.

"Stay in a secret place," Jonathan warned David. He promised to learn his father's plans and to report them to his friend.

David summed up his chances in a few sad words. "There is but a step between me and death."

Deep in the woods, the two friends worked out a code for communicating with each other. If anyone else was near, Jonathan would use the code to alert David.

"Hide behind the stone heap in the field," Jonathan repeated the code. "And I will shoot three arrows toward it, as though I shot at a mark. Then I will send the lad to find the arrows. If I say to him, 'Look, the arrows are on this side of you, take them,' then you can come, for, as the Lord lives, it is safe for you and there is no danger."

The other part of the code was the alert. David listened as his friend underscored the danger. "But if I say to the lad, 'Look, the arrows are beyond you,' then go; for the Lord has sent you away."

Once again the two friends parted as Jonathan made a farewell pledge: "The Lord stand witness between us forever to the pledges we have exchanged."

The next day brought the Feast of the New Moon. At this religious festival everyone in the court was expected to feast at the king's table. Jonathan was there. So was Abner, commander of the king's army. And so were all the officers of the court. David's seat was empty.

On the second day of the feast David's seat was again vacant. King Saul could no longer ignore the empty seat. He turned to Jonathan. "Why has not the son of Jesse come to the meal, either yesterday or today?"

Jonathan had thought out his answer, with help from David. He told his father, "David earnestly asked leave of me to go to Bethlehem." He explained that the family of Jesse planned to attend a special religious service in that city.

This answer unloosed a tirade from the king. "As long as the son of Jesse lives upon the earth, neither you nor your kingdom shall be established," the king fumed. "Send and bring him to me, for he shall surely die."

"What has he done?" Jonathan pleaded for his friend. "Why should he be put to death?"

The king then became furious. He seized his spear and hurled it toward his son in disgust. Jonathan never flinched. He had his answer. The king's mind would not change. Sadly, Jonathan went to tell David.

The plan went as they had outlined it. Jonathan walked into the woods, taking a little boy with him. He carried a bow, as though he would practice shooting arrows. Stopping near a spot where David hid behind the mound, Jonathan let three arrows soar into the air.

"Run," he cried out to the little boy. "Run and find the arrows which I shoot." Jonathan called loud enough for David to hear him. "Look, the arrows are beyond you. Hurry! Stay not! Make haste!"

The boy gathered up the arrows, little dreaming that he was part of a plan between two desperate friends. Jonathan thanked his helper and sent him back to the city.

David came from behind the stone heap. He fell on his face to the ground and bowed humbly once, twice, three times to honor the prince who was risking his own life to help him.

The two friends kissed and wept together, their tears mingling in their grief. Both knew the choices before them. David must leave. Or he must die. And between them lay the unspoken reality: They might never see each other again.

David sent his farewell to his bride. He dared not risk a return to his house.

"Go in peace," Jonathan said. "The Lord shall be between me and you, and between my descendants and your descendants, forever."

Jonathan returned to the house of his father, the king. David turned his steps toward the opposite road. The son of Jesse was now an outcast. His star that once showed such brilliance now dimmed. He took the route that led to his beginning—toward the rugged hills of Judah.

9.

In Exile

David stayed a step ahead of death.

The barren hills of Judah abounded in numerous rocky caves. These were perfect places for fugitives hoping to disappear from sight. David headed toward them, hoping to find refuge. His most pressing needs were food and a weapon to defend himself. He went to a city called Nob and stopped at a holy sanctuary for help.

"Why are you alone and no one with you?" the chief priest, Ahimelech, asked David. Ahimelech was a great-grandson of the prophet Eli.

David thought up a quick answer. The king had put him in charge of a serious matter, David told Ahimelech. Everything had to be done in secret. In his haste, there was no time to pack needed supplies. "Give me five loaves of bread, or whatever is here," David asked.

The only food available was holy bread, which the priests were allowed to eat when new loaves replaced the old. The only weapon at hand was the sword of Goliath, sent to the sanctuary for safekeeping. The priest gave the bread and sword to David.

The ancient cave of Adullam provided an underground asylum in the early days of David's exile. From there he managed to get word to a few key people. David knew that King Saul would track him down. He needed to attract a small band of men to be with him.

The group that came made an interesting mixture. Some of the men were David's kinsmen from Bethlehem. Some were warriors who had fought under

David in the army. There were also restless men who came, searching for adventure. And some were desperate men, running from the law.

To these men David offered a promise. He would train them to be skillful warriors and provide for them. But David also exacted a promise from them. They must be loyal to one another and to him. And above all else, they must be willing to follow wherever he would lead them.

Jesse of Bethlehem brought his household to join his son in exile. David's father was afraid that the king, in his anger, would harm his family in order to punish his youngest son. David knew that his parents were too old for the rigors of the vagabond life he would have to lead. He went to the king of Moab, the native country of his great-grandmother Ruth.

"Pray let my father and my mother stay with you, till I know what God will do for me," David requested.

The king of Moab granted David's wishes, and his parents lived peacefully in Moab throughout the years of David's exile.

From his hiding place, David sent out spies to keep him informed of the events at King Saul's court. The spies found out that the king planned a campaign to capture David. Another fugitive brought news that made David fall prostrate in tears and remorse. King Saul's own spies learned how the priest had given David food and a weapon. The king called together everyone from the sanctuary. He refused to listen to their explanation that Ahimelech had no way of knowing that David was a fugitive.

In one of his uncontrollable moods, the king ordered that Ahimelech and all the priests at the sanctuary be executed for treason. And every man, woman, child, and animal in Nob, the city of priests, was put to the sword. The deed reaffirmed David's understanding of the unsettled condition of King Saul's mind.

One person escaped the massacre of the priests. Ahimelech's son, Abiathar, managed to get away and fled to find David.

"Stay with me," David told Abiathar, "Fear not; for he that seeks my life seeks your life; with me you shall be in safekeeping."

The incident reminded David how dreadful his own fate would be if the king ever caught up with him. He felt partly responsible for the death of the innocent priests.

At such times David poured out his feelings in poetic phrases. In all his sorrows, in all his hardships, David kept his unshakable faith that he would be guided toward a noble destiny.

> But I am like a green olive tree
>   in the house of God.
> I trust in the steadfast love of God
>   for ever and ever.
> I will thank thee for ever,
>   because thou has done it.
> I will proclaim thy name, for it is good,
>   in the presence of the godly.
>
> Psalm 52:8-9

David's scouts also brought word that the dreaded Philistines were attacking the Israelite city of Keilah, not far from his hideout. Praying for guidance from God, David took his followers, now numbering about six hundred, and raced to rescue the beseiged city. They soundly defeated the Philistines.

News of this daring rescue reached King Saul. Since Keilah was a walled city, the king decided to hurry and trap David before he could get out. "God has given him into my hand," the king said, "for he has shut himself in by entering a town that has gates and bars."

King Saul summoned his soldiers to war, to go down to Keilah and capture David.

Warned of the king's movements, David and his men slipped out of the city and fled to the thick woodland of the hill country, in the wilderness of Ziph. And the king continued to search for him.

It was in the wilderness, at Horesh, that the king's son came in secret to visit the fugitive. Prince Jonathan brought words of encouragement to his friend. "Fear not; for the hand of Saul my father shall not find you," he said to David. "You shall be king over Israel and I shall be next to you."

Before they parted the two steadfast friends made a covenant before the Lord. For one last time they embraced and wept at the thought of parting, but vowing their friendship forever. David remained in the wilderness. Jonathan went home.

David kept on the move, always eluding the king. Deeper and deeper into the wilderness he moved his men, making their homes in caves and in thick forests. The life was rough. Yet, the months in the wilderness taught David a resourcefulness he would never have learned as a member of King Saul's court. He learned how to be tough and how to show compassion. And he developed confidence in his ability to do any task that needed to be accomplished.

Even King Saul grudgingly gave David praise for his skill in eluding him. "David is as crafty in his hiding places as a jackal," the king told his soldiers.

The crafty outlaw and his band roamed the wilderness of Judah. In order to get food and clothing they exacted tributes from wealthy men in return for protecting caravans and farms from raiding tribes.

At last they came to the wild wilderness of Engedi, known as the Wilderness of the Wild Goats. Jackals and wild goats roamed at will among the steep rocks.

The caves of Engedi sprawled in intricate patterns, with caves within caves. In one of the inner caves David found a temporary home for his band. It was there that King Saul finally got a glimpse of him.

The king happened to be returning from a successful bout with the Philistines. When he learned that David hid in the wilderness of Engedi, he decided to find him. The king selected some of his best fighters and went to hunt for the fugitive among the rocks of the wild goats.

David saw him coming. From the innermost parts of his hideout he spied King Saul and his soldiers making their way toward the cave. Keeping out of sight, David watched as they neared the cave and the king left his troops. Walking alone, King Saul went into the cave to refresh himself.

One of David's men came up beside him and whispered a reminder. "The Lord has put your enemy in your hand."

David hushed the speaker. King Saul was still the anointed king of Israel, and the father of Jonathan and Michal. Never must David lift his hand against him. Once a king had been anointed, he was looked upon as a sacred person.

Instead, David moved toward the king. Reaching from the darkness of the cave he snipped off a piece of the king's robe.

Then he motioned to his men and led them through the winding cave to a safe spot high on a hill. A deep chasm separated them from the king and his army.

David waited until the king emerged from the cave. "My lord the king!" he called out.

The king recognized David's distinctive voice. "See, my father," David called again, "see this piece of your robe in my hand. By the fact that I cut off the skirt of your robe and did not kill you, you may know that there is no wrong or treason in my hands." David closed his moving speech by saying, "May the Lord judge between me and you!" He promised never to lift his hand against King Saul.

The king wept. In an emotional voice he spoke to David across the chasm. "You have repaid me good, whereas I have repaid you evil." The king then ended his speech by asking David to grant a surprising favor. "I know that you will become king, and that the kingdom of Israel shall be established in your hand," he said. "Swear to me by the Lord then that you will not exterminate my descendants and blot out my name from my father's house."

David swore this to the king.

As suddenly as they came, King Saul and his soldiers went home. But David felt with certainty that the king would come looking for him again. In his unpredictable mind, King Saul hated him one moment as an enemy, and in the next moment he loved him as a son.

David knew that he must stay in exile.

10.
Abigail

Samuel came to the end of his days. And with the death of the prophet, an old story surfaced and spread. The story was about David.

While David was still a shepherd boy, the story revealed, the prophet had a vision. In the vision he was directed by God, "Fill your horn with oil, and go. I will send you to Jesse the Bethlehemite, for I have provided for myself a king among his sons."

Samuel said, "If Saul hears of it, he will kill me." So he pretended to go and conduct religious services. The moment he saw young David the prophet said, "This is the one!" He took the holy oil and anointed David as the future king over Israel. But those who witnessed the anointing kept it a secret, fearing for the life of Samuel—and for their own lives if King Saul learned of it.

With the spread of the story, the king redoubled his efforts to find David and eliminate him. All these happenings were told to David in exile, and he became more determined to stay alive.

He had developed a system of survival for himself and for his band of outlaws, which now included practiced warriors. He protected farmers, herdsmen, and caravan leaders from raids by bands of roving marauders. In return David and his men received a portion of the farm produce, sheep and goats. David's brigands also made raids of their own, taking only from the rich.

Nabal was a rich farmer. He owned three thousand sheep, one thousand goats, and huge farms and orchards. He also had a beautiful wife named Abigail.

David protected Nabal's sheep, and at the season for shearing, he made sure that the shearers were protected also. One day David sent ten young men to talk with Nabal.

They were very polite. "All good wishes for the year ahead!" they began. "Prosperity to yourself, your household, and all that is yours!"

David's men then reminded Nabal how they had helped him. "Pray, give whatever you have at hand to your servants and to your son David." they requested.

Now Nabal was as mean and churlish as he was

ABIGAIL

rich. "Who is David?" he asked in an insulting
manner. "In these days every slave who breaks away
from his master sets himself up as a chief."

Nabal sent nothing but insults.

David answered the insults in a six-word steely
command. "Every man gird on his sword!"

Four hundred fighters buckled on their swords and
followed their leader. Two hundred stayed behind to
watch over their belongings.

While this was going on, one of Nabal's servants
reported his surly behavior to Nabal's wife, Abigail.
She took control of the situation. Without a word to
her husband, she hurriedly collected supplies of food.
She packed loaves of bread, sheep dressed for roast-
ing, bunches of raisins, cakes of dried figs, along with
parched grain and a supply of wine. All these she
loaded upon donkeys.

"Go on before me," Abigail told her servants. "I will
come after you."

On her way to meet David she met him coming to
punish her husband. She fell at his feet, bowing low to
the ground. "Let me take the blame, my lord," she
pleaded. She apologized for her husband's behavior
and begged David not to give vent to his anger. "If any
man sets out to pursue you and take your life, the Lord
your God will wrap your life up and put it with his
own treasure, but the lives of your enemies he will
hurl away like stones from a sling." She went on
pleading with David not to give way to his feelings and
kill her husband.

Abigail talked until David's temper cooled. He
revealed his gentle side. "A blessing on your good
sense," he said softly. "If you had not come to meet
me, not a man of Nabal's household, not a single
mother's son, would have been left alive by morning."

He accepted her gifts and gave her a gentle farewell.

"Go up in peace to your house; see, I have hearkened to your voice, and I have granted your petition."

The two strong personalities were destined to meet again. When Abigail reported her actions to Nabal he went into such a rage that he had a seizure, falling like a stone. He never recovered and died ten days later.

David never forgot Abigail's thoughtfulness and intelligence. He let time pass, then sent messengers to her farm. This time the message was totally different from the first one. "David has sent us to you to take you to him as his wife," the message said.

Abigail consented. "Your handmaid is a servant to wash the feet of the servants of my lord," she answered.

She joined David as his wife, bringing with her many servants, cattle, and great wealth. David knew that King Saul had declared an end to the marriage with Michal, and she had been given to another man in marriage.

Soon after this David faced another crisis. His spies reported that King Saul was on his way with three thousand chosen men. He had learned of David's present hiding place in the wilderness of Ziph, in Judah near the great Salt Sea.

David's scouts tracked the movements of the king's mighty host until the king set up camp on a hill beside a road in the wilderness.

Then David decided to be his own spy and visit the camp. He took along one soldier, a kinsman named Abishai, who volunteered for the dangerous assignment. Deep in the night the two men sneaked up to the camp where everyone was sleeping. Even the sentries had dozed.

David and Abishai crept to the center of the encampment. They saw King Saul, asleep with his spear stuck in the ground near his head. All around the king the soldiers lay in a deep sleep.

"Let me strike him and pin him to the earth with one thrust of the spear, and I will not strike him twice," Abishai said.

"Do not destroy him," David commanded. Instead, he took the king's spear and a jar of water. They left as quietly as they came. No man saw them. No man awoke.

At the first hint of early morning, David climbed up the side of a mountain ovelooking King Saul's camp. A deep ravine between them gave him safety. As he had done once before, he called out and reminded the king how he had spared his life.

"Is this your voice, my son David?" King Saul asked.

"It is my voice, my lord, O king," David reassured him. Then he asked, "What have I done? What guilt is on my hands? The king of Israel has come out to seek my life, like one who hunts a partridge in the mountains."

The king's attitude softened. "I have done wrong," he cried out. "Return, my son David, for I will no more do you harm, because my life was precious in your eyes this day."

David answered his king, "Behold, as your life was precious this day in my sight, so may my life be precious in the sight of the Lord, and may he deliver me out of all tribulation."

The king's last words carried a blessing. "Blessed be you, my son David! You will do many things and will succeed in them."

David went back to his hiding place. King Saul returned home.

David longed to go home behind the king. For the time being King Saul seemed to have sincerely forgiven him. From experience, however, David knew how quickly his moods could shift from love to hate and back again.

David said in his heart, "I shall perish one day by the hand of Saul."

As long as he was within the borders of Judah, whether in wilderness or cave, there was the danger that the king could capture him.

So David made a momentous decision. He would cross the border and go into the land of the Philistines. He trusted his cunning to keep him alive there until he could return home.

11.

A Refuge in Gath

David approached the walled city of Gath, known as the city of splendor. Of the five city-states of Philistia, Gath was the one nearest to Judah.

David's scouts had already let him know that he would receive a cordial welcome. His followers waited outside the city gates while he went in alone to talk with Achish, ruler of Gath.

Within a short time David's charm had captivated Achish, as it did so many people. The Philistine leader explained that they had a mutual foe in King Saul. He suggested that they work together for their mutual protection.

The two leaders came to an agreement. Achish, ruler of Gath, offered David and his followers a place of refuge. In return, David, leader of a strong fighting unit accustomed to dealing with desert raiders, would help to keep the borders of Gath safe.

David brought his troop into the city, and for a time all went well. But he saw that his people felt as strangers among the unfamiliar customs and the worship of strange gods. They needed a place of their own.

Undaunted, David went to Achish with another request. "If I have now found favor in your eyes," David said, "let a place be given me in one of the country towns, that I may dwell there."

Achish gave David the country town of Ziklag, on the border of Judah. After years of homeless wandering, David and his followers could finally put down roots for a time. They marched into Ziklag, taking their wives and children and all their belongings.

David took two wives. In addition to Abigail, he had married a young girl named Ahinoam. A leader of David's stature was expected to have several wives.

David kept his part of the bargain with Achish. He helped him to ward off raiding attacks, and sometimes took his men on forays of their own against various tribes. David pretended that the raids were mostly against territories of Israel. Instead, he attacked tribes such as the Amalekites and other constant enemies of his people. They often returned with herds of sheep, goats, food, weapons, and clothing. Some raids brought riches in the form of expensive ornaments. The booty was shared with Achish, and sometimes with the people of Judah. David wanted to make sure that he kept the good will of the powerful tribe of Judah. He might need their support one day.

A year and more passed. Achish made plans for David to stay near him permanently. A bond of friendship had developed between the two men.

David wisely kept his own plans secret. He knew

that he walked a tight-rope existence. On the one hand, he pretended to be a loyal vassal to Achish. On the other hand, he kept spies who reported movements among the soldiers of King Saul, as well as he kept spies among the Philistines. One day the report from spies forced David to face his dreadful dilemma. The armies of the Philistines were about to begin an all-out campaign to destroy the armies of Israel.

David knew he would be forced to choose sides. He weighed his choices as he went to face the ruler of Gath. Achish assumed that David would welcome a chance to defeat King Saul. "You assuredly know that you will go out with me to battle, you and your men," he said.

David was caught in a web. He was obligated to the Philistine leader for giving him refuge. If he refused to join their fighters, he would be considered a traitor. He weighed this fact against the thought of fighting against Israel—against Jonathan.

David hedged for time. "Surely," he said, "you know what your servant can do."

Achish accepted this as a willingness to fight with him. "I will make you my bodyguard for life," he promised David.

Hard pressed, David called upon the God he trusted.

> Preserve me, O God,
> for in thee I take refuge.
> Thou dost show me the path of life.
>
> Psalm 16:1,11

David rallied his own warriors, all the while hoping for a miracle. To the loud blast of trumpets, the combined Philistine forces began to assemble. The sight was fearsome to behold.

Charioteers zipped past in their horse-drawn vehicles, each chariot equipped with scythe-sharp blades. Companies of archers held their bows poised for action. Endless columns of foot soldiers marched in precision. And with them all the Philistine lords and princes passed in review.

David and his unit joined the rear guard as directed by Achish. As they began advancing, David was still hoping for a way out of his dilemma.

Unexpectedly, the Philistine commanders saved him. When they saw David's unit they rebelled in anger. "What are these Hebrews doing here?" they asked.

Achish tried to explain. David had been with him for more than a year. "I have had no fault to find in him ever since he came over to me," he said in reassurance.

"Send this man back," the commanders insisted, pointing to David. "He may turn traitor in the battle."

Disappointed, Achish spoke to David. "Return now, and go on in peace."

David, a magnificent actor, feigned disappointment. But inwardly he realized that he had been saved from a fate too horrible to imagine.

He set out with his men for the long trip back to Ziklag. As they approached the town a horrible sight marred their homecoming. Gone were the familiar landmarks. There was only blackness against the sky. Homes had been reduced to charred hulks. Smoke still curled upward from the devastated ruins.

There was no sign of life.

David's cry of desolation was joined by the weeping of his warriors. They all wept until they could weep no more.

Then David suddenly galvanized into action. First, he asked Abiathar, the priest, to offer a prayer for guidance. Then without stopping to rest, he called to his men to follow.

In the desert they came upon an Egyptian slave, half dead from hunger. After David fed and revived the slave, the young man told them what happened.

The Amalekites had swooped upon Ziklag, burning and looting. They pillaged the homes, set fire to the town, and carried off the women, old men, and children—even the animals.

David's actions spoke his commands. Two hundred men who were too tired to move stayed behind to keep watch. The others followed David toward Amalek.

They came upon the Amalekites, where they had set up a temporary camp. They were singing and dancing in celebration of their victory and the abundant spoils of warfare.

David struck without warning. With the fury of a death-defying desert storm he attacked them. All through the night and the next day David and his men punished the culprits. The only men who escaped were those who managed to reach their camels and ride away into the desert.

After the fighting, David and his faithful men recovered everything that the Amalekites had stolen. The women, the children, the animals, and household goods were returned to Ziklag. Along with these things was added a wealth of gold and silver taken from the Amalekites.

Everything was divided. Some of the riches went to Judah, along with a message from David: "This is a present for you from the spoil of the enemies of the Lord."

A dispute arose among the weary men when the remainder of the spoil was divided. Should those who stayed behind to watch receive as much as those who went to fight?

David settled the matter with a firm announcement. "For as his share is who goes down into the battle, so shall his share be who stays by the baggage; they shall share alike." This was a law he established to govern those he ruled. "Share and share alike."

12.
"How Are the Mighty Fallen!"

David waited in Ziklag for news of the battle. While he helped to rebuild the town, he waited.

How was King Saul's army faring against the Philistine mighty forces? He wondered. And what of Jonathan? From past experience David knew that Jonathan would be on the front lines.

A part of the story of the battle David would learn at a much later time. That part concerned King Saul.

Even before the battle began, the king had doubts. And when he saw the mighty fighting machine of his enemy, he did not know where to turn.

The frantic king took off his crown one night and went in disguise to visit a woman who claimed to predict future events. She lived at a place called Endor and was famed for her ability to communicate with the spirit of the dead. People called her the Witch of Endor.

King Saul sat before the Witch of Endor and asked a favor, believing the woman did not know his identity. "Divine for me by a spirit, and bring up for me whomever I shall name to you," the king said.

"Whom shall I bring up for you?" the Witch of Endor asked.

The king whispered a name that had been in his thoughts for years: "Samuel."

When the spirit of the prophet appeared, King Saul began speaking. "I am in great distress," he cried out. "The Philistines are warring against me, and God has turned away from me and answers me no more, either by prophets or by dreams; therefore I have summoned you to tell me what I shall do."

The spirit of Samuel relayed to King Saul a prophecy more chilling than the one which the prophet had given at their last meeting. "Tomorrow you and your sons shall be with me."

At these words the king fell full length upon the ground in fear. All strength left his body. In his mind, the upcoming war was already lost.

Details of this meeting along with word of the battle, would reach Ziklag later. For the present David waited and hoped.

After three days of waiting the news came. The people of Ziklag spied a strange man coming toward the town at full speed. As the stranger came closer they noted that his complexion carried the swarthy and sunburnt hue of a desert nomad.

David and his followers braced for the news he brought, for the runner's clothes were rent. Dirt covered his head. The torn clothing and dirt-smeared head were symbols of woeful tidings.

The stranger, utterly exhausted, prostrated himself at David's feet.

"Where do you come from?" David asked.

"I have escaped from the camp of Israel," the runner answered.

"How did it go?" David's voice drew taut with suspense and eagerness. "Tell me."

The man told him. The story gushed out, broken by choking, gasping sobs. As the stranger talked, David could picture clearly the scenes described, the dreadful battle between King Saul's army and the Philistine forces.

They clashed along the slopes of a mountain, Mount Gilboa. The Philistines charged up the slopes in a mighty assault, showering death along their path. Chariots and horses crushed the Israelite soldiers beneath their might. Spears and arrows flew through the air as though blown by a storm.

Jonathan and his brothers fought bravely. Abner, the commander in chief, tried to keep his troops together. But from the beginning the tide of battle flowed against them. They were no match for the Philistines with their larger army and superior weapons

"The people have fled from the battle, and many of the people also have fallen and are dead." the messenger continued. His next words hit David with the force of a thunderclap. "And Saul and his son Jonathan are also dead."

Perhaps the stranger was mistaken. "How do you know that Saul and his son Jonathan are dead?" David asked.

"By chance I happened to be on Mount Gilboa," the man assured him. He told how Jonathan refused to retreat, even when the battle seemed lost. Though the prince had been wounded many times by archers, he fought to the death, protecting the escape of the commander and trying to save his two brothers.

And King Saul?

The true account of King Saul's death would not be revealed until later. This is how it probably happened.

Badly wounded by archers, the king pleaded with his armor-bearer to kill him and prevent the enemies from capturing him and bringing further shame to Israel. "Draw your sword and thrust me through with it," he pleaded.

The armor-bearer could not bring himself to kill his

king. So it was that King Saul ended his own reign. He remained ruler of Israel until the end of his life. No one took his kingdom away from him. Drawing his royal sword, he pointed it toward his heart, fell upon it, and died.

That was one account. The story told to David by the stranger was different. The man no doubt hoped to curry favor if David ever became king.

King Saul did not die at once, the stranger recounted. As King Saul lay wounded, he called out to the stranger. "Who are you?" the king asked.

"I am an Amalekite," the stranger answered.

The king begged a favor of the Amalekite. "Stand beside me and slay me; for anguish has seized me, and yet my life still lingers."

The Amalekite described his actions for David. "So I stood beside him and slew him, because I was sure that he could not live after he had fallen." At this point the man held out a crown toward David, saying, "And I took the crown which was on his head and the armlet which was on his arm, and I have brought them here to my lord."

At the sight of the crown David acted as though he had lost his mind. He tore his clothes as he cried out in sorrow. His fury and grief turned upon the bearer of the woeful tidings. How dare this man, an alien, an Amalekite, lift his hand against an anointed king? In his unreasoning grief, David ordered one of his men to put the runner to death.

David sentenced the courier. "Your blood be on your own head; for out of your own mouth you condemned yourself when you said, 'I killed the Lord's anointed.'"

Then David lifted his voice in loud lamentation. His warriors came and cried with him. They refused to eat, fasting and weeping together until nightfall. David cried for King Saul, who in the strength of his young years started Israel toward greatness. He cried for his friend, Jonathan, who had risked his own life that David might escape and stay alive. And David cried for Israel, the nation now without a leader.

The mighty had fallen!

David poured out his sorrow in poetry. His song of lament honored Jonathan and King Saul and Israel. And as he sang the words and played his harp, the strings wailed in doleful harmony. Even the harp strings seemed to be weeping with David.

"Thy glory, O Israel, is slain upon
thy high places!
How are the mighty fallen!
Tell it not in Gath,
publish it not in the streets of
Ashkelon;
lest the daughters of the Philistines
rejoice,
lest the daughters of the
uncircumcised exult.

"Ye mountains of Gilboa,
let there be no dew or rain upon
you,
nor upsurging of the deep!
For there the shield of the mighty
was defiled,
the shield of Saul, not anointed
with oil.

"From the blood of the slain,
from the fat of the mighty,
the bow of Jonathan turned not
back,
and the sword of Saul returned not
empty.

"Saul and Jonathan, beloved and
lovely!
In life and in death they were not
divided;

they were swifter than eagles,
　they were stronger than lions.

"Ye daughters of Israel, weep over
　　Saul,
　who clothed you daintily in scarlet,
　who put ornaments of gold upon
　　your apparel.

"How are the mighty fallen
　in the midst of the battle!

"Jonathan lies slain upon thy high
　　places.
I am distressed for you, my brother
　　Jonathan;
very pleasant have you been to me;
　your love to me was wonderful,
　passing the love of women.

"How are the mighty fallen,
　and the weapons of war
　　perished!"

2 Samuel 1:19-27

David called the elegy the Song of the Bow. He asked that it be taught to all the citizens of Judah. "Let it echo and re-echo throughout Israel," he said.

This was David's final tribute to his steadfast friend, Jonathan the prince.

13.

King David

David said good-bye to Ziklag and Achish and crossed over into Judah. He returned to the territory of his clan. When David came to Judah he did not know what events would shape the direction of his life. He brought his two wives, Abigail and Ahinoam. And he brought his band of warriors, along with their families.

David waited and prayed for guidance.

One day the chief elders of Judah came to him. They needed a leader, the elders said. David was their kinsman. He had a strong fighting unit. So the elders invited him to be their king. The elders assembled at Hebron, the capital city of the tribe. They anointed David as king over the house of Judah.

David looked like a king. He was now thirty years old. Weather and the years on the desert had tanned his skin. His quiet eyes were still as keen as when he watched for prey in the pastures, but they now held faint crinkles at the corners. His reddish beard added to the majesty of his appearance.

One of the new king's first acts was to compose a message to a group of heroic men. After the defeat at Mount Gilboa the Philistines had hung the bodies of King Saul and his sons in one of their cities and made them objects of scorn.

But brave Israelites from Jabesh-gilead remembered that when Saul first became king he had saved their people from becoming slaves to the Ammonites. So men from Jabesh-gilead traveled all night and took down the bodies, at the risk of their own safety. They burnt the bodies and buried the bones at Jabesh, under the kind of tree King Saul loved—a tamarisk tree.

In his message David thanked the heroes and gave them words of inspiration. "Be strong, and be valiant; for Saul your lord is dead, and the house of Judah has anointed me king over them."

While this took place, another king was being crowned. Abner, commander of King Saul's army, had escaped from Gilboa. He set a younger son of the dead king to rule as king over the house of Saul. The king, Ishbosheth, was only a figurehead. Abner was in control.

There were now two kings. Ishbosheth ruled over most of the northern tribes. He lacked experience and the ability to inspire, and his kingdom grew weaker, while David's grew stronger.

Finally Abner realized that the people could only be united under one king. David agreed to talk with Abner, but he set the terms. Abner could not come into his presence without bringing Saul's daughter, Michal.

Abner agreed and persuaded Ishbosheth to take Michal away from her present husband and return her to David. In addition the shrewd commander spoke with the elders of Israel, persuading them that David should be their king also.

Then he went to see David. "I will arise and go, and will gather all Israel to my lord the king, that they make a covenant with you, and that you may reign over all that your heart desires," Abner declared.

David thanked the commander and granted him a safe conduct home. But meanwhile, Joab, David's nephew, who was also his army commander, found out about the meeting. Joab met Abner at the city gate and killed him. Abner had earlier killed one of Joabs brothers in self-defense.

The deed infuriated David. He not only berated Joab, but brought down a curse upon him and his descendants. Then he ordered the people to mourn for Abner, who was buried at Hebron. At the grave David sang a lament for the warrior who had spent his life fighting to keep Israel's enemies at bay.

"Should Abner die as a fool dies?
Your hands were not bound,
your feet were not fettered;

as one falls before the wicked
you have fallen."

2 Samuel 3:34

With Abner dead, King Ishbosheth was left at the mercy of ambitious soldiers. One day while he slept, two of his own captains came into his house and murdered him. After this tragedy the elders came to David. They chose him to be "shepherd and prince" of all Israel.

When the Philistines learned of this, they challenged David's power. They were afraid of waiting until he organized a stronger army.

The new king answered by putting together the combined forces of Israel and Judah to soundly crush the Philistines. Israel's ancient nemesis was never again strong enough to prove a threat.

There were other, more peaceful matters for David to handle. His family had grown at Hebron. His first wife, Michal, had joined him. And sons were born to his other wives. The son of Ahinoam was the oldest. He was Amnon. Abigail's son, Daniel, lived but a short time. A third son, Absalom, and a daughter, Tamar, were children of Maacah, daughter of the king of Geshur. A fourth son, Adonijah, was born to a wife named Haggith. A fifth son, Shephatiah, was the child of Abital, and the sixth, Ithream, the son of a wife named Eglah. A strong king such as David was expected to have many wives and many strong sons.

David was a man with a compassionate heart, and he loved his children dearly. He loved them to the point of spoiling them. He could easily discipline six hundred tough grown men, but he could never bring himself to punish any of his children. And since most of them had different mothers, they grew up with differing beliefs and behavior patterns, depending upon the upbringing of their mothers.

This fact was destined to eventually bring heartache to the House of David.

14.

The City of David

The old city rested upon hard limestone rock, which mounted into two majestic heights: Mount Zion and Mount Moriah. Across a natural valley rose the beautiful Mount of Olives.

It was a fortress city, called "the stronghold of Zion." The city was better known as Jebus, or Jerusalem. The inhabitants were a racial mixture of people called Jebusites.

King David chose the city as a perfect site for a capital to further unite the various tribes into one nation. Geographically, the city was fairly central to all tribes.

There was a problem, however. The Jebusite city had been impregnable for centuries. High above sea level, it commanded a view of highlands and lowlands. A stout wall of solid stone defied attack. Above the city wall rose towers from which guards kept watch from all sides.

When the Jebusites heard that David wanted their city they vowed he would never enter it. So strong was their fortress, they boasted, that their blind and crippled people could guard it.

David never let obstacles stand in his way. Every defense system usually had a weakness, he reasoned.

He sent Joab to take some of their best spies to find a weakness. Some of the spies entered the city disguised as pilgrims, and some as traders. Others came pretending to be beggars.

Inside the city walls the spies discovered a possible weakness: the water system. The source of water for the city was a natural spring, too low to be enclosed within the city wall. A narrow tunnel cut into the rock allowed the water to flow under the hill. Within the city wall a vertical shaft, or gutter, reached down into the tunnel to bring the water to the people.

David used this engineering secret to plan his attack. Under cover of darkness, Joab led volunteers who inched their way up the slippery shaft. The first man up let down ropes to aid the others waiting below.

Once inside the city these volunteers overpowered the sentries at the gate before they could sound the alarm. Then the gates were thrown open to David and his forces waiting outside.

The city was captured from within. And with its capture David influenced the course of history for all years to come. The new capital became "The City of David."

Strict orders from David protected the Jebusites. Those who stayed were allowed to keep what they owned; those who left did so in peace.

David planned that the new capital would become a religious as well as a political center. He appointed two chief priests. One was the faithful Abiathar, who had followed David during his years in exile. The other was a former Jebusite priest named Zadok.

As part of the religious revival, David planned to bring the Ark of the Covenant into the new capital. His big dream was to eventually build a magnificent temple to house the Ark.

Joy overflowed the city the day the Ark was finally

brought to Jerusalem. Skilled musicians organized groups to play every type of musical instrument known to them.

The Ark rested on a new cart pulled by oxen. Priests marched ahead blowing their long straight trumpets. The musicians blended the clarinets and castanets and clashing cymbals. These were accompanied by the playing of lutes and harps and the blowing of horns and trumpets.

There were dancers. David the king led the dancing. Dressed in pure white linen he leaped and whirled for joy.

When the Ark was securely in a tent, the people joined in a religious ceremony. After that David blessed the people and gave each man and woman in the multitude a gift of food—a loaf of bread, a portion of meat, and a cake of raisins.

David the king gave thanks to the Lord:

Sing to the Lord, all the earth!
Tell of his salvation from day to day.
Declare his glory among the nations,
his marvelous works among all the peoples!

1 Chronicles 16:23-24

15.

Growth and Progress

David talked with Nathan the prophet about his dreams for Israel. And Nathan, a friend as well as an adviser, gave sound counsel.

"Do all that is in your heart, for God is with you,"

Nathan said. He urged David to be practical and to do those things that needed to be done first. Other tasks, such as the building of a temple, could wait.

Taking his friend's advice, David began a practical building program. Homes were needed for the officials, citizens, and workers who wanted to move to the capital. Also, a home was needed for the king.

Hiram, king of Tyre, offered help. Hiram was impressed with David's aggressive leadership. His rich kingdom on the Mediterranean had much to offer. King Hiram sent loads of cedar wood to build a palace for David and his growing family. He sent not only building materials but craftsmen as well.

A nation moving toward greatness needs national security. David modernized and reorganized a standing army. In former years Israel's fighting host was made up largely of men who were mobilized when the need for fighting arose. David organized an army of professional soldiers.

In addition to the regular standing army, David organized a personal unit, his bodyguards. These men took the place of the old "runners" or "messengers." Many in this unit were foreigners, soldiers of fortune, who made loyal guards. They held no strong allegiance to factions in the kingdom and were fiercely loyal to David.

Another major task for David was the expansion of trade and commerce. Israel was still poor. Fortunately, the kingdom stretched along the path of key trade routes. One route, the Way of the Sea, ran from Egypt, along the Mediterranean, to the coast of Phoenicia, a land of merchants and transporters. A well-traveled caravan highway, the Way of the King, stretched to Damascus, a wealthy trading city. Crisscrossing these routes were other highways that formed a network of lanes for travel and trading. Kingdoms that controlled trade routes could gain wealth from collecting taxes.

As David's army defeated one kingdom after another—Amalek, Edom, Philistia, Moab, Ammon, and Syria—Israel gained access to or control over vital trade highways. Many nations were not conquered but thought it best to form friendly alliances with David. The conquered nations, as well as those needing David's protection, offered costly tributes. This swelled the national treasury. Israel expanded in both wealth and size.

The capital city also expanded. The original Jebusite city was only about ten acres in area, and hemmed in on three sides by ravines. To add space, Jebusite engineers had constructed terraces along the slopes, with foundations of earth and rock. The architectural feat was called the Millo. With the help of Phoenician engineers, David enlarged the Millo. He also made the Millo secure from erosion. The city of Jerusalem continued to grow.

As a sensitive poet, David realized the importance of history and the arts to a nation of people. He introduced new ideas. A position of "royal scribe" was added to the important people of his court. The close association with Phoenicians introduced their way of written communication. The Phoenicians had refined the Egyptian hieroglyphic system, which used countless word-signs. The Phoenician alphabet used only twenty-two signs, which could be combined to form consonant sounds. In later years the Greeks added vowel sounds.

With the new Phoenician alphabetic writing, words and ideas could be recorded as never before. David's keen intellect recognized the revolutionary impact.

The royal secretary, or scribe, was a Phoenician named Sheva. It was Sheva's duty to handle all of David's letters and messages. Sheva also taught other people of the court the new system of writing. Under his instructions, the ability to read and write spread from Jerusalem to other places.

Music flowed through the palace as naturally as the water in the spring outside the city wall. Singers were organized to delight and inspire listeners, and instrumentalists were trained to accompany them. The atmosphere was one of joy and splendor.

> So David reigned over all Israel;
> and David administered justice and equity
> to all his people.

2 Samuel 8:15

David the king kept the image of greatness before his subjects. Israel had grown from an oppressed nation, with enemies on all sides, to become one of the leading nations of the world.

The king wrote poems about it. He said prayers of thanksgiving for it. And his singers rang out the theme in their music.

> "What other nation on earth
> is like thy people Israel?"

1 Chronicles 17:21

16.

Bathsheba

King David stepped out on his palace roof.

It was late afternoon, at the height of the hot season. Jerusalem lay still and sweltering. As day came to a close the king sought a spot where a cool breeze might blow.

He also wanted solitude, away from the bustle of life in the palace. So he came to his favorite spot, overlooking the trees and gardens. Despite the heat, there was beauty everywhere he looked, and David loved beauty in all forms.

From the parapet he could look far across his beloved city. Because of his building program, stone houses—small ones and mansions—dotted the hills. As lingering rays slanted upon the slopes, the stone houses reflected a soft, rosy glow, as if the whole city blushed from a day-ending sun-kiss.

A breeze sprang up, brushing the king's cheeks, calming his weariness. He relaxed in the solitude on the rooftop. He thought he was alone.

A slight movement on the roof of a nearby house caught his attention. Someone was moving about.

The king stood watching.

A maidservant came out and stepped on the roof next door. She stooped and filled a pottery basin with water, then disappeared as quietly as she had come.

In the next moment a young woman came out. Little suspecting that anyone watched her, the young lady unpinned her hair, shaking the strands to let the curls cascade upon her shoulder. Then in the near-darkness she began to bathe.

David watched her, curious at first, then fascinated. In the last glow of the sun-painted evening she seemed as lovely and delicate as an almond blossom. The king made up his mind to find out more about her.

One of the royal servants gave the information the king needed. "Bathsheba," the servant said the name. "Bathsheba, the daughter of Eliam, the wife of Uriah the Hittite."

David learned more. Bathsheba's grandfather was a well-known elder of Judah. Her husband, Uriah, was a skilled warrior. He was at that very time fighting with the king's army under Joab, the commander in chief.

This information should have alerted David to the danger of further thoughts on Bathsheba. But all his

life he had found challenge in the seeming unattainable. He fell deeply in love with the enchanting woman, and she returned his love. Only her husband stood in the way. So David began to scheme.

David sent word to Joab, his commander. "Send me Uriah, the Hittite."

Uriah came at David's bidding. When he returned to the fighting lines the king gave him a sealed message to take to his commander. Uriah thought that the message contained directions for battle plans.

What the soldier really took was his sealed death sentence.

"Set Uriah in the forefront of the hardest fighting, and then draw back from him, that he may be struck down and die." This was David's instruction to Joab.

It happened as the king commanded. Joab was a true soldier and carried out the command exactly as ordered. Uriah was killed by a hail of arrows from enemy archers.

Bathsheba mourned for brave Uriah. She believed her husband's death was due to natural war casualty. So did most other people. When the customary period of mourning was over, David sent for Bathsheba. She became his wife.

In his heart David knew the great shame of his deed. He was troubled. He had broken sacred laws. In all his years in exile, and as king, he had never stooped to such an act.

He sent for Nathan, his friend and adviser. When the prophet came he told the king a story, a parable.

There were two men in a certain city, the one rich and the other poor. The rich man had very many flocks and herds; but the poor man had nothing but one little ewe lamb which he had bought. And he brought it up, and it grew up with him and with his children; it used to eat of his morsel and drink from his cup, and lie in his bosom, and it was like a daughter to him.

Now there came a traveler to the rich man, and he was unwilling to take one of his own flock or herd to prepare for the wayfarer who had come to him, but he took the poor man's lamb, and prepared it for the man who had come to him.

2 Samuel 12:1-4

After the telling David cried out in anger, "That man should die!"

"You are that man," Nathan told him. Then he began to scold the king for taking the only wife from Uriah and sending him to his death. Nathan was the only person in all the kingdom who had nerve enough to scold the king. He reminded David that he would be punished.

Nathan's voice filled the room, sounding a dire prophecy upon the house of David: "Now therefore the sword shall never depart from your house. . . ."

David cried out with shame. "I have sinned against the Lord."

His friend pitied him. "The Lord has put away your sin," he said. "You shall not die." David would live, Nathan said, but the first child born to Bathsheba and David would die.

And it happened. The baby was born sickly. David prayed night and day, asking the Lord to forgive him and spare the child's life. The king refused to eat or drink as long as the baby lay ill. At last a servant brought the sorrowful news. The child was dead.

All of these happenings affected David deeply. He was never again the gay, spirited king he had always been. He prayed a great deal, and in his writings he repeatedly asked forgiveness for his sin.

Have mercy on me, O God,
  according to thy steadfast love;
according to thy abundant mercy
  blot out my transgressions.
Create in me a clean heart,
  O God,
  and put a new and right spirit
    within me.

Later, a second son was born to David and Bathsheba. Nathan named the boy Jedidiah, meaning
beloved of Yahweh, beloved of the Lord.

Bathsheba, the mother, knew of the curse, "The
sword shall never depart from your house." So she
gave the child a gentle name—Solomon, the peaceable
one. And by this name the son was known.

Again and again, David sang his pleas for
forgiveness:

Blessed is he whose transgression is forgiven,
  whose sin is covered.
Blessed is the man to whom the Lord imputes no iniquity,
  and in whose spirit there is no deceit.

I acknowledged my sin to thee,
  and I did not hide my iniquity;
I said, "I will confess my transgressions to the Lord";
  then thou didst forgive the guilt of my sin.

Psalm 32: 1-2, 5

17.

The Sword in the House

David and his kingdom settled down to a period of
well-deserved peace. There were no wars to command

his attention. Borders were secure. Trade routes were open and busy. Trained officials carried on many of the daily duties of government.

There was time to reflect upon his personal life. In these reflections David thought a great deal about Jonathan. He had never forgotten the promise he made to the prince, to care for his descendants forever. Many times David had searched, but the search always proved fruitless.

Now that his kingdom was secure, he began anew, sending scouts far and near. "Is there still anyone left of the house of Saul that I may show him kindness for Jonathan's sake?" he inquired.

One scout found a young man, a cripple named Mephibosheth. He was indeed Jonathan's son, living in hiding. When Jonathan died the son was a baby. In haste to hurry the baby into hiding, his nurse had dropped the child, making him a cripple for life.

David sent for Mephibosheth. He came to the palace, fearful that he would be killed. He threw himself at the feet of the king.

David spoke gently. "Do not fear," he said. "I will show you kindness for the sake of your father Jonathan, and I will restore to you all the land of Saul your father; and you shall eat at my table always."

Mephibosheth still suspected a ruse. "What is your servant that you should look upon such a dead dog as I am?" he asked. Jackals were plentiful in the area, and the sight of a dead dog or jackal symbolized lowliness, the worst of sights.

David understood. To show his sincerity he gave to the crippled son all the possessions that once belonged to King Saul. In addition, servants and a steward were appointed to care for Mephibosheth all the days of his life. And Jonathan's son ate at King David's table as one of the king's sons.

The king's oldest sons were now grown and living their own lives. His daughter, Princess Tamar, was the darling of the court. Her exquisite beauty and lovable ways won the hearts of those around her. Both Tamar and Absalom inherited unusual features from David and their mother, Maacah, a Geshurite.

Amnon, the oldest son, grew up reserved and secretive. He loved Tamar, but not in a brotherly manner. In some of the nearby kingdoms it did not seem unnatural for a brother to love or marry a sister. The famed Egyptian rulers King Akhenaton and Queen Nefertiti were brother and sister. However, the custom was not practiced in Israel.

One day Amnon pretended to be sick and asked his father to permit Tamar to visit him. "Pray let my sister come and make a couple of cakes in my sight," the prince asked.

David consented, for Tamar was an excellent cook. The princess obeyed. But when she took the cakes to her brother, Amnon forced himself upon her.

Tamar ran crying to Absalom, who tried to comfort her. "Now hold your peace, my sister," he whispered. But to himself he vowed to get even with his half-brother.

David was furious with Amnon, but he did not know how to handle the problem. Had it been a military or political matter he could have dealt with it immediately. But he never learned how to discipline his own children. So he did nothing. And the result was tragic.

Absalom waited. When it was time for the Feast of Sheepshearing, he planned a gay celebration. David had given to each son a large herd, and Absalom raised his sheep at a farm about fifteen miles from

Jerusalem. He invited his father and brothers to come to a grand feast there.

David could not go, but he sent the other sons with his blessing. For a time there was feasting and merrymaking among the brothers. Then suddenly Absalom flashed a signal to a servant. Before anyone could stop him, the servant pounced upon Amnon and killed him. The other princes, fearing that they would all be killed, mounted their mules and rode away.

In the confusion that followed, Absalom and his servant escaped. They traveled until they reached the kingdom of Absalom's maternal grandfather in Geshur, east of the Sea of Galilee.

Meanwhile, a garbled account of the murder reached the king. "All of the princes have been murdered!" the report stated.

David reeled in shock. Later news that Amnon alone was dead could not lessen his pain. He tore his clothes in grief and fell to the floor, mourning for his sons.

For three years Absalom stayed in Geshur. David, and no one else, could grant him pardon and a safe return home. Even though the king longed each day to see his favorite son, he refused to consider his return.

The king seemed to grow old overnight. With one prince murdered and the other in exile he knew that the prediction of Nathan was coming to pass: "The sword shall never depart from your house."

Joab, the faithful commander, thought of a plan to revive the king's spirits. Absalom should come home. But each time Joab broached the subject, the king refused to listen.

So Joab sent to Tekoa for a wise woman to help him with a solution. Joab coached the woman in what to do and the words to speak. "Behave like a woman who has been mourning many days for the dead," he instructed.

Following Joab's instructions, the wise woman of Tekoa came to David. The king was hearing cases and giving out judgment.

"Help, O king," the wise woman cried, falling upon her face before David.

"What is your trouble?" the king asked.

"Alas, I am a widow; my husband is dead." The woman began her tale. "I had two sons. One of them struck the other and killed him. And now, the whole family has risen against your handmaid, and they say, 'Give up the man who struck his brother, that we may kill him. . . .' " Before she finished her story the king understood the moral of the parable. He was convinced to bring his son home.

Absalom arrived, expecting a warm welcome from his father. He was wrong. David issued a stern order: "Let him dwell apart in his own house; he is not to come into my presence."

The prince was stunned. For two years he tried to see his father. Still David kept his son exiled in his house, away from the palace. The king did not want his people to think that he had fully pardoned Absalom. They might demand further punishment for the prince.

Finally, Absalom was permitted to come to the palace. David embraced his favorite son and kissed him.

Absalom was free to travel about again. So he resumed his arrogant ways. He acquired a flashy chariot. Since the defeat of Syria, chariots had become popular in Israel.

Each day Absalom rode through the narrow streets of the capital, his whip snapping and the horses prancing. His luxuriant hair fanned out as he whizzed past. Fifty bodyguards ran before the chariot to clear the way. The people were impressed by the dazzling sight.

Absalom rode to the city gate, the public meeting place of a town or city. The handsome prince greeted the people, those coming and those leaving. He listened to their problems and their complaints. Many citizens showed anger because the king and his judges were too slow in giving them justice in legal matters.

Absalom sympathized. "Oh, that I were judge in the land!" he said. "Then every man with a suit or cause might come to me, and I would give him justice." The prince had an embrace and a kiss for each person who spoke with him.

Absalom, the prince, worked out a plan he had nurtured during his years in Geshur. Slowly, with infinite patience, he was stealing the loyalty of many of David's subjects. But this was only part of a major plan.

With the next step, Absalom would try to seize the entire kingdom from his father, the king.

18.

"My Son, My Son"

"As soon as you hear the sound of the trumpets, then say, 'Absalom is king at Hebron!'"

The signal from the prince alerted his supporters in Israel. They must be ready. Absalom was about to seize the kingship.

A runner arrived at David's palace with the startling message. "The hearts of the men of Israel have gone after Absalom."

The news hit David like a thunderclap. He had given Absalom permission to go to Hebron with two hundred people. They went for a special religious feast, he thought. Now David knew that his son took the crowd to organize an attack against his throne.

Heartstricken as he was, the old warrior of many battles took command of the crisis. Later news let him know that his son planned to march against the capital. As a military tactician, David realized the danger of having his army trapped in a walled city. Beyond that, he did not want his beloved Jerusalem to become ravaged as a battleground.

David issued rapid-fire commands. "Arise, and let us go, or else there will be no escape from Absalom." The king's faithful servants and soldiers reassured him of their loyalty. "Your servants are ready to do whatever our lord decides."

David decided to organize a network of spies to keep him informed about events in the capital. The chief priests, Abiathar and Zadok, could move about and not be suspected. Each of the priests had a son who was a swift runner. The priests could pass secrets to their sons, who in turn could relay the information to David.

The king's own guards ran up and down the streets to alert the citizens and fighting men. At the sound of the rams' horns, all who were loyal to David were to assemble outside the city gate on the highway to the east.

The king's spirits lifted when he saw the thousands who passed by in review. Among the troops he noted that there were hundreds of foreigners. He called to one, a soldier named Ittai.

"You are a foreigner, and an exile from your home," David said. He urged Ittai not to risk the uncertainty of going with him.

The soldier intoned his answer with the fervor of a litany. "As the Lord lives, and as my lord the king lives, wherever my lord the king shall be, whether for death or for life, there also will your servant be."

The priests came, pulling the Ark with them. In the early days of Israel their ancestors had usually kept the Ark before them in times of danger.

David agreed at first, then changed his mind. "Carry the ark of God back into the city," he said. "If I find favor in the eyes of the Lord, he will bring me back and let me see both it and his habitation; but if he says, 'I have no pleasure in you,' behold, here I am, let him do to me what seems good to him."

The journey began with prayer services. David arranged a meeting with a very old and very wise leader named Hushai. The wise man waited at the summit of the Mount of Olives, beside an ancient stone where pilgrims came to pray and ask protection for a journey.

David led his multitude up the slopes to the altar. They walked with bare feet, their heads covered in mourning. As they prayed at the altar, none knew if they would ever see their beloved city again. They sobbed as they prayed, and the king cried with them.

Hushai, the old man, prepared to follow David when they came down the slopes. David stopped him. "Return to the city," he pleaded. Hushai must pretend to be faithful to Absalom, David advised. In this position he could work with Abiathar and Zadok as agents.

David and his followers then marched to the banks of the Jordan River to wait for word from his intelligence network. Swift runners brought the information they needed. Absalom had not expected his father to leave the capital. The surprise left him uncertain and hesitant.

It was here that wise Hushai played his part. He advised Absalom to wait.

This gave David the precious time he needed. He crossed the Jordan to the walled city of Mahanaim, in the territory of Gilead. There the army set up headquarters.

The loyal Israelites of Gilead rounded up supplies for the soldiers. They supplied beds, basins, earthern vessels, wheat, barley, meal, parched grain, beans, lentils, honey, cheese, and meat.

As more soldiers came to join David's headquarters, he organized them into three companies, with a commander over each. Joab, Abishai, and Ittai each commanded one of the three major divisions.

"I myself will also go out with you," David told them.

"You shall not go out," his commanders answered him. "If half of us die, they will not care about us. But you are worth ten thousand of us."

So David stood at the city gate and saw his soldiers march away to battle. He called aside his commanders and gave a poignant plea. "Deal gently for my sake with the young man Absalom."

The commanders understood. Absalom was to be defeated. But the king's favorite son was not to be killed.

The king's army surprised Absalom's forces in the forest of Ephraim, beyond Jordan. The battle raged through the thick forest, and over the face of the countryside.

In the end, Absalom's soldiers sensed defeat. They began to scatter into the hills. Absalom leaped upon his mule and tried to escape. Those who saw him thought he hoped to find his way to Geshur again.

As the prince galloped through the forest, his long, thick hair became tangled in the branches of a great oak tree, holding him fast. The mule under him ran on, leaving Absalom dangling by his hair.

A soldier saw him and remembered the king's plea. He refused to kill the prince, but ran to tell Joab.

Joab never hesitated. Most of his life had been given to winning security for Israel. If Absalom lived, Joab knew that David would probably forgive his son, leading to more civil strife.

Joab walked to the prince and aimed three darts so that they could not miss Absalom's heart. Soldiers buried the prince in the forest.

Then Joab blew his ram's horn. The fighting was over.

Runners swiftly returned to the city gate. "All is well," the first runner called to David.

The king's anxiety came in his question. "Is it well with the young man Absalom?"

The first runner could not bear to answer. So the king repeated the question. "Is it well with the young man Absalom?"

The answer from the second runner left no doubt. "May the enemies of my lord the king, and all who rise up against you for evil, be like that young man."

David turned and covered his face with his hands. Rocking back and forth in anguish, he cried for his favorite son.

> "O my son Absalom,
> My son, my son Absalom!
> Would I had died instead of you,
> O Absalom, my son, my son!"
>
> 2 Samuel 18:33

What might have been a victory celebration turned into a time of mourning. Joab arrived upon the sad scene as the king still mourned over and over, "O my son Absalom, O Absalom, my son, my son!"

For the first time in his long years of faithful service Joab lost patience with David. The commander's voice cut cold as steel as he reminded the king that soldiers had risked their lives to save his kingdom. Yet, David sat thinking only of his dead son.

"Now, therefore arise," Joab cried out. "Go out and speak kindly to your servants."

The shock therapy worked. David went to stand at the city gate and thank his gallant soldiers. But in his heart he never forgave Joab for killing Absalom while he hung helpless.

The king's troubles were not yet ended. Pockets of resistance still lingered in the capital, and in the territory of Judah as well. These rebellious groups were finally quieted with the help of faithful Joab, though David had stripped him of his position as commander. Joab was later restored to the command that meant so much to him.

And David the king returned to the city he loved.

19.

Looking to the Future

David never fully recovered from the shock of Absalom's rebellion. The people of his court watched with sorrow the rapid decline of the king's health.

Despite his weakening condition the king continued to plan for the future of Israel. Rulers of lesser vision would have been content to rest upon the accomplishments that seemed sufficient for several kings.

David had guided Israel from a struggling pastoral community into a strong kingdom equal to any other in the East. Israel's borders were extended and secure, so that the vision of the Promised Land had finally been realized. The recording of Hebrew history had been advanced to a point far beyond any imagined attempts.

But there remained other tasks. One major project proved more innovative and daring than most of David's myriad visionary schemes. He decided to number his people. For the first time there would be a census to determine who was actually in his realm.

Such a venture, especially if never done before, required immense organizational and administrative skill. In addition, the people being numbered had to be convinced that a census was necessary. This was not an easy task to ease the fears of people who had never been numbered before.

The immediate reaction of the people was anger. God had not ordained David to number the people, they said. It was Satan who was inciting the king to do so. The tribal elders saw the act as another example of the weakening of their control over the people. These elders did not look kindly upon a strong centralized government.

David went ahead with the census, which he felt was necessary in planning for the future. Up to then nobody had the slightest idea of how many people were in the realm, or what their ages might be.

Joab was given the task of supervising his soldiers in the numbering. And even Joab did not like the idea. He advised the king against it. "May the Lord your God add to the people a hundred times as many as they are, while the eyes of my lord the king still see it; but why does my lord the king delight in this thing?" Joab emphasized the last part of the question.

David listened. But Joab was overruled. So he left with his officers to count the people. The gigantic project took nearly a year. Joab and his men traveled up and down the realm. They crossed to Jordan, toward Gad and then to Jazer, then to Gilead, as far as the fortress city of Tyre and to all the cities of Hivites and Canaanites. And they went out to the Negeb of

Judah at Beer-Sheba. They covered all the land and came back to Jerusalem after nine months and twenty days.

It was unfortunate that an epidemic of sickness swept over Israel as the census was being completed. People saw it as punishment because of David's decision to number them. When thousands and thousands of people died even David became frightened.

A story was told as to why the punishment came in the form of an epidemic. According to the telling, David was given three choices of forms in which the punishment would come. The word came through a seer. The first choice of punishment was three years of famine in the land. The second choice was defeat, with three months of flight and the enemy close behind. And the third choice was the three days of pestilence in the land. So the third choice came to pass.

With the census completed and the epidemic ended, David turned to the task that was dear to his heart. All during his reign he dreamed of it, the building of a temple to the glory of God. Nathan, the prophet, had wisely advised David to leave the task to a king who would reign in more peaceful times. And David agreed, but this did not keep him from thinking about the project and planning for it. As his wealth increased he had continually set aside some of it toward this end. Now that his land was tranquil, David began to plan the details of the temple in earnest.

He even chose the site, for it had appeared to him in a dream. To the north of Jerusalem rose a slab of rock that had long been a holy place of worship for the Jebusites. A Jebusite named Araunah owned the land surrounding the high rock. He had built upon the land a threshingfloor.

David went to the farmer and explained his need for the place. The farmer graciously offered the land as a gift, but the king preferred to pay fifty shekels of silver for the site. There he built an altar. And there the temple would one day stand on the majestic Mount Moriah.

20.

The Star Still Shines

Who would build the temple? The question was uppermost in David's mind. He had become weary and feeble. Which of his sons would be wise enough to carry out his plans?

No definite rules for succession had yet been established. David was only the second king of Israel. King Saul died before he was given a chance to name a son. Now David could decide the person to follow him to the throne. There was no law that said it had to be the oldest son.

Already the struggle for succession had begun behind the scenes. Adonijah was the oldest surviving son. But there was young Solomon, whose mother, Bathsheba, remained the king's favorite wife. The great love between David and Bathsheba never seemed to lessen as they grew older.

Adonijah promoted himself, saying, "I will be king." He began to act as though he was already king. He acquired chariots and horses and rode through the streets daily with fifty drivers riding before him. The prince was nearly as handsome as Absalom had been, and many people said he looked the way David looked as a young man.

Members of the king's court naturally took sides. Adonijah? Or Solomon?

Joab, the commander in chief, gave his support to the oldest son. So did Abiathar, the high priest. On the other hand Zadok, the other high priest, favored Solomon. Another strong supporter for the younger son was Nathan, who had helped to train Solomon and teach him wisdom as he grew up.

David remained silent.

The matter came to a head when a bout of illness put David to bed. The king's strength seemed to be ebbing day by day.

Seizing the initiative, Adonijah planned a special feast. He invited Joab, Abiathar, and most of his brothers. He did not invite Solomon, nor any of his brother's supporters.

The festivities took place at a stone beside the spring called En-rogel, a traditional place of worship. The prince invited a host of friends, including officials from Judah, where there was strong support for Adjonijah. Hundreds of oxen, calves, and fatted sheep were prepared.

It was rumored that during the sacrificial feast Abiathar, the priest, would anoint Adonijah with holy oil as the self-appointed king. Then messengers would be sent to proclaim the news that Adonijah was the new king of Israel.

Rumors about the scheme reached Bathsheba and Nathan in the palace. Despite his anger over her in the beginning, the beautiful, intelligent woman had won the friendship of the prophet. Now the two friends worked out a plan to help Solomon.

Bathsheba went in to talk with the sick king. There was not time to lose. She bowed low and did obeisance.

"What do you want?" asked David.

She answered, "My lord, you swore to your maid-servant by the Lord your God, saying, 'Solomon, your son shall reign after me, and he shall sit upon my throne'." Bathsheba then told him the news about Adonijah.

At this point, as they had arranged, Nathan joined Bathsheba beside the sick king. The prophet described the rumored anointing of Adonijah and told how the people were already shouting, "Long live King Adonijah!"

Hearing these words some of the fire of warrior days flashed into David's eyes. To Bathsheba he swore an oath. "As the Lord lives, who has redeemed my soul out of every adversity, as I swore to you by the Lord, the God of Israel, saying, 'Solomon your son shall reign after me, and he shall sit upon my throne in my stead'; even so will I do this day."

Bathsheba's answer carried love and respect. "May my lord King David live forever!"

Sick as he was, David planned the ceremony, and in a short time. So it was that a procession left the palace and headed for another spring, the Gihon. Young Solomon rode upon his father's ceremonial royal mule. Leading the way were soldiers of the royal guard. Following were Zadok, Nathan and Benaiah, who was captain of the guards. Behind marched the heralds, holding their rams' horns ready.

At Gihon Spring the young prince Solomon knelt before the priest Zadok, who took the horn of oil and anointed him king.

At this signal the chorus of rams' horns blared the news. Trumpets underscored the tidings. "Long live King Solomon!" the heralds cried out.

The people of Jerusalem heard their cry and took up the words of triumph: "Long live King Solomon!"

In the palace the weakened king heard the sound

and rejoiced. "Blessed be the Lord, the God of Israel, who has granted one of my offsprings to sit on my throne this day, my own eyes seeing it."

With Solomon on the throne, David improved in health and devoted his time to planning the temple. Each detail was planned with love, for he knew that Solomon would carry out his father's dream.

David revealed to the new king all the treasures he had stored up to build the temple. "With great pains I have provided for the house of the Lord a hundred thousand talents of gold, a million talents of silver, and bronze and iron beyond weighing. . . ."

And David said to Solomon his son, "Be strong and of good courage, and do it. Fear not, be not dismayed, for the Lord God, even my God is with you."

The old king knew that he was nearing the end of his days. "Our days on earth are like a shadow," he said, "and there is no abiding." He had reigned seven years as king of Judah, and thirty-three years over all Israel. And as he contemplated the end of his long fruitful life, he constantly asked forgiveness for any sins committed during his lifetime. He was not a perfect man. David admitted this to himself, to his friends, and in his writings.

Perhaps the Psalms, those that are attributed to David, and any he may have inspired, would become his noblest monument. In his Psalms he displayed his love for God, his compassionate nature, and recognition of his imperfections. Only a man of nobility could do this.

When the time of David's death drew near, he called his son, King Solomon, to him. It was to Solomon he looked to carry on all that he had started.

"I am about to go the way of all the earth," David told Solomon. "Be strong, and show yourself a man."

And among the last words of David are poetic

phrases to guide any ruler, or any person with authority over another.

> The God of Israel has spoken,
>   the Rock of Israel has said to
>   me:
> When one rules justly over men,
>   ruling in the fear of God,
> he dawns on them like the morning
>   light,
>   like the sun shining forth upon a
>   cloudless morning,
>   like rain that makes grass to
>   sprout from the earth.
>
> 2 Samuel 23:3-5

So David the king went to rest with his forefathers. He was buried in the city of David. His lineage would stretch down through the centuries. And the Star of David would continue to shine for all years to come.